IMAGES
of America
HATTIESBURG

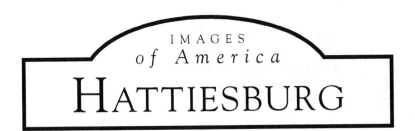

IMAGES
of America
HATTIESBURG

Brooke Cruthirds and Colter Cruthirds

ARCADIA
PUBLISHING

Copyright © 2013 by Brooke Cruthirds and Colter Cruthirds
ISBN 978-1-5316-6768-9

Published by Arcadia Publishing
Charleston, South Carolina

Library of Congress Control Number: 2012955099

For all general information, please contact Arcadia Publishing:
Telephone 843-853-2070
Fax 843-853-0044
E-mail sales@arcadiapublishing.com
For customer service and orders:
Toll-Free 1-888-313-2665

Visit us on the Internet at www.arcadiapublishing.com

*To Yvonne Arnold and Iola Williams, for their inspiration and their
commitment to preserving Hattiesburg history*

CONTENTS

Acknowledgments   6

Introduction   7

1.   Hattiesburg's Founding Father   9

2.   Rails and Lumber   23

3.   Industry and Growth   37

4.   Educational Institutions   53

5.   Camp Shelby   69

6.   City Life   89

7.   Rural Scenes   119

ACKNOWLEDGMENTS

Though this book is, in many ways, the product of the community it represents, the authors would like to acknowledge a few people who had a particular hand in its completion. The images included here are derived from both public and private collections. Those from private collections have only been included here with granted permission. The staff at the McCain Library & Archives at the University of Southern Mississippi was a tremendous help—especially Lisa Jones, Diane Ross, Cindy Lawler, Amanda McRaney, and Elizabeth La Beaud. Likewise, we are thankful to Sherry Laughlin and Reese Powell at the William Cary University Library. Chad Daniels, Christy Calhoun, and Michael Rucker of the Mississippi Armed Forces Museum generously donated their support, time, and expertise. Many thanks go to Latoya Hathorn for her continued dedication at the African American Military History Museum and to Deborah Denard Delgado for the love she has devoted to her community. Special thanks go to Michael P. Fedoroff, for his friendship and interminable work ethic, and to Simone Monet-Williams, Jason Humphrey, and the rest of the staff at Arcadia Publishing for their assistance (and patience) in the production of this volume.

Finally, the authors would like to acknowledge the Hub City historians who have already produced fine work on the area and have made our path that much easier to walk. Specifically, we would like to thank Tony Howe for his work with the Mississippi Great Southern Chapter of the National Railway Historical Society, Nollie W. Hickman for *Mississippi Harvest*, Frank Brooks for his booklet *Traveling by Trolley in Mississippi*, Kenneth G. McCarty for his book *Hattiesburg: a Pictorial History*, and Gilbert Hoffman for his excellent works *Steam Whistles in the Piney Woods* and *Dummy Lines Through the Longleaf*.

INTRODUCTION

Though it might seem that Forrest County was so named as a misspelled homage to the virgin forests of longleaf pines, which grew upwards of 150 feet and in such density that the landscape appeared forbidding to early settlers, it is in fact the namesake of Nathan Bedford Forrest, a Confederate lieutenant general in the American Civil War and the first grand wizard of the Ku Klux Klan. Ironically, Nathan Bedford Forrest never settled in the area, and no major battles of the American Civil War were fought here. Still, the name is apt: like General Forrest, the county's history has been shaped by innovation, tenacity, and racial controversy. Like General Forrest, the development of Hattiesburg, the county's largest city and seat of government, was directly impacted by the scars of that war.

Hattiesburg, with a population of 46,000 and counting, is home to the University of Southern Mississippi, William Carey University, Camp Shelby, and a host of national manufacturing companies. It is often affectionately called "Hub City" because of its geographical relationship to six other distinctly Southern cities. The railways and highways fan out from Hattiesburg, like spokes on a wheel, to Meridian, Jackson, Natchez, New Orleans, Gulfport, and Mobile.

Compared to some of the cities on the rim of this great wheel, Hattiesburg is not very old. Even in the early 19th century, when Natchez, New Orleans, and Mobile were already well-established centers of commerce and trading, Hattiesburg had not yet been carved out of the virgin longleaf pine forests. Only a few white travelers—mostly on their way to Mobile to sell produce or skins—had set foot on this land. Until the early 19th century, the forests of the Pinehills region were home to an estimated 20,000 Choctaws who, aside from fashioning trees felled with hand-made axes into dugout canoes, left the woods unscathed. As John Claiborne described it in 1840, "For twenty miles at a stretch in places you may ride through these ancient woods and see them as they have stood for countless years, untouched by the hands of man, and only scratched by the lightening or the flying tempest."

The Choctaws were displaced by the Treaty of Mount Dexter of 1805. White settlers migrated to the area from surrounding counties; some were interested in establishing truck farms, and some had realized the potential value of the forests. The early white settlers established log cabins and trading posts along the banks of the Leaf and Bouie Rivers and from the remaining Choctaw in the area, learned how to cure meat and preserve fruits and vegetables.

The settlement, which came to be called Twin Forks because of its location on the two rivers, was very much a frontier, fraught with all of the thievery and murder associated with life on the fringe. The Copeland clan perpetrated a "reign of terror" from Jackson to Mobile and were well known for swindling—or outright robbing—pioneers of the Twin Forks area. James Copeland, dubbed the "Great Southern Land Pirate," was finally captured after a bloody shoot-out in Perry County (southwest of Hattiesburg) in which he and his gang had intended to avenge his partner's death. Copeland successfully killed his partner's killer but was later caught in Mobile County and served four years there for thievery. After his stint, Copeland was extradited to Perry County, tried, and hanged for murder in 1858. He was buried on the banks of the Leaf River, but his body was stolen two or three days later. Copeland's skeletal remains were reportedly displayed at McInnis & Dozier Drugstore in Hattiesburg until the early 1900s.

That a ruthless criminal would be transformed into window dressing for a downtown drugstore seems to fit in quite nicely with the history of Hattiesburg's beginnings. Despite any frontier difficulties, the land had an undeniable economic draw; where some saw a vast, untamed wilderness, others saw money. The first sawmills sprang up in this area in the 1840s, and the timber industry—though not yet in full bloom—was budding. Sawmills at this time were dependant on rivers to transport timber (the felled trees were lashed together into rafts and floated downstream to the mills), so loggers were restricted to cutting trees along the riverbanks.

A number of innovations changed the logging industry in the last quarter of the 19th century: circular saws replaced reciprocating saws, crosscut saws replaced axes for felling trees, and dry kilns dramatically cut the time it took to produce usable lumber. The most dramatic change to Hattiesburg's burgeoning lumber industry came on steel tracks and was powered by steam engines.

By 1900, railways gave Hattiesburg access to Meridian, Jackson, New Orleans, Mobile, and Gulfport—important gateways that drastically expanded domestic and foreign markets. In addition, lumber companies created their own "dummy lines" in order to address the depleted forests near streams and rivers; railroads allowed sawmills to profit on timberland that had previously been inaccessible. The lumber industry in Mississippi was now in full bloom. Within the first decade of the 20th century, the state ranked third in lumber production (behind Louisiana and Washington), and as much as 80 percent of the state's total output came from sawmills in the aptly named Pine Belt.

Sawmills offered good-paying jobs for any man who was willing to work hard, and a number of towns developed around this industry—Lumberton (literally "Lumber Town"), Sumrall, Wiggins, Laurel, and Picayune, to name a few. However, none of these towns enjoyed the benefits of the railroad to the extent that Hattiesburg did. The intersection of the railways put Hattiesburg in something of a cartographic crosshairs that fostered the growth of its educational institutions, allowed manufacturers to ship their products worldwide, and attracted the establishment of one of the largest military training bases in the United States.

This book begins with the founding of Hattiesburg by William H. Hardy, and moves from there to the impact of the lumber industry and the railroads, to the educational institutions that benefited from the largess of the local timber tycoons, to the development and growth of Camp Shelby, to scenes of city and rural life in the 1920s. This book focuses on the founding and early years of Hattiesburg and by no means pretends to be a complete history; it does not cover Hattiesburg's important and controversial role in the Civil Rights Movement, its designation as the "birthplace of Rock and Roll," or the Project Dribble nuclear testing of the 1960s. Rather, it is the authors' sincerest hope that this photographic survey of Hattiesburg's early years will inspire residents to take an active interest in the history of their city.

One

Hattiesburg's Founding Father

Capt. William Harris Hardy, a lawyer, engineer, and veteran of the Civil War, conceived the idea of a railroad connecting New Orleans to New York with the belief that linking vital commercial centers could reunite the country and help the South recover from the devastations of the war. Hardy spent the next 12 years surveying, planning, and promoting his proposal.

Local legend has it that in August 1880, Captain Hardy stopped for lunch at a clearing surrounded by a large oak and several hickory trees on the north side of Gordon Creek. Reportedly, he took a nap and dreamt that this area—with its fertile soil and climate congenial to agriculture—would be an ideal site for a city. It was here that Hardy spread a map of the South and, studying the Meridian–New Orleans railway line, drew another line connecting Gulfport and Jackson. These proposed lines, which intersected in the forest at the place where he was sitting, must have seemed like an X on a treasure map, for Hardy immediately decided to locate a railroad station on that spot. The resulting town was named in honor of his second wife, Hattie.

By 1883, the first train ran from Meridian to Hattiesburg; a year later, the tracks across Lake Pontchartrain to New Orleans were completed. In 1900, the first train ran from Jackson through Hattiesburg to Gulfport. Not coincidentally, Captain Hardy was responsible for platting two other cities in Mississippi: Gulfport and Laurel. These three cities are connected by Hardy's railroads, and each has had tremendous impacts on the growth and development of the others. For instance, both Hattiesburg and Laurel began as lumber towns, while Gulfport provided a major port for the delivery of the lumber from those cities to expansive national and international markets.

Though the Hattiesburg area was already rich in natural resources, it is highly unlikely that this city would exist in its current form if Captain Hardy had not napped (and dreamed) on a pleasant summer day along the banks of Gordon Creek.

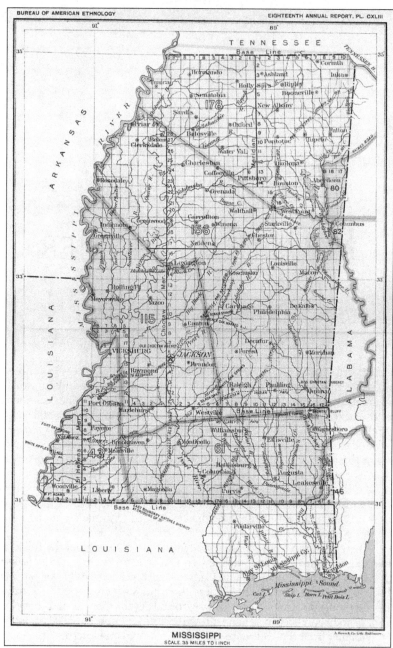

MISSISSIPPI
SCALE 35 MILES TO 1 INCH

This 1899 view divides the state of Mississippi by Native American land cessions. Forrest County is located squarely in territories ceded by the Choctaw Nation according to the Treaty of Mount Dexter in 1805. An estimated 20,000 Choctaws once inhabited the area now known as Forrest County, and early white settlers learned many life-sustaining skills from them, such as curing meat or preserving fruit. (Photograph courtesy of the Mississippi Armed Forces Museum.)

Captain Hardy, an engineer, lawyer, and veteran, believed that railroads would reunite the country and help the South recover from the devastation of the Civil War. He was appointed to lay a right-of-way for the Gulf & Ship Island Railroad. In August 1880, Hardy and his survey team stopped for lunch and rest along the banks of Gordon Creek (what is now downtown Hattiesburg). Hardy napped and, when he awoke, told his engineers that he had dreamed of a future city at the spot they were now surveying. (Photograph courtesy of the University of Southern Mississippi McCain Library & Archives.)

William Harris Hardy (1837–1917) was born in Todds Hill, Alabama. He received his formal education at Town Creek Academy and, later, at Cumberland University in Lebanon, Tennessee. In 1855, when he was but 18 years old, he founded the Sylvarena Academy in Flowers, Mississippi. He taught at Sylvarena for a year before moving to Raleigh, Mississippi, where he took and passed the bar exam and began his legal career. He would continue practicing law until his death. In 1861, he joined the Confederate army as a captain. (Photograph courtesy of the University of Southern Mississippi McCain Library & Archives.)

William H. Hardy met his first wife, Sallie Ann Johnson, at the 1859 State Fair in Jackson, Mississippi. Hardy was enamored by her beauty and later said that he had fallen in love with her at first sight. They married in 1860 and had six children: Mattie, Willie, Ellen, Elizabeth, Thomas, and Jefferson Davis. (Photograph courtesy of the University of Southern Mississippi McCain Library & Archives.)

This 1862 letter from a homesick William H. Hardy was handwritten to his first wife, Sallie, during his days in the Confederate army. Hardy, in Lynchburg, Virginia, expresses his concern for his pregnant wife, writing: "I long to get home now. I never have before given myself any uneasiness about you, but I must confess that I am now greatly uneasy for your welfare . . . Do try and content yourself if possible till I get home and then if it be in my power to do so, I will make you happy . . . If you have to suffer, why I'll use every means in my power to get my resignation accepted and return to you at once." Hardy served in the Confederate army from 1861 to 1865, when complications from a gastric ulcer forced him to return home. (Photographs courtesy of the University of Southern Mississippi McCain Library & Archives.)

This c. 1872 picture shows William Hardy after he moved to Meridian, Mississippi, to set up a law firm there. He made the move after his first wife, Sallie, died in 1872, having contracted what was called "malignant malaria" while tending to victims of an outbreak of the disease in the couple's hometown of Paulding, Mississippi. (Photograph courtesy of the University of Southern Mississippi McCain Library & Archives.)

Hattiesburg is the namesake of Hattie Hardy (née Lott), William Hardy's second wife. William met Hattie in her native Mobile, Alabama. She is said to have been affable, and it is perhaps this quality that drew the widower Hardy to her so quickly. After a brief courtship, they married on December 1, 1874, and Hattie moved to Meridian with William and helped him raise his six children. In addition to the six children from Hardy's first marriage, Hattie and William had three more: Lena Mai, Lamar, and Toney. Hattie died in 1895, having never set foot in the town named for her. (Photograph courtesy of the University of Southern Mississippi McCain Library & Archives.)

THE UNITED STATES OF AMERICA,

To all to whom these presents shall come, Greeting:

Whereas _____ W. Hardy, _____ County, _____

_____ in the GENERAL LAND OFFICE of the United States a CERTIFICATE OF THE REGISTER OF THE LAND OFFICE at _____

_____ Full Payment has been made by the said William H. Hardy _____ according

to the provisions of the Act of Congress of the 24th of April, 1820, entitled "An Act making further provision for the sale of the Public Lands," and the acts supplemental thereto, for

_____

_____

according to the Official Plat of the Survey of the said lands, returned to the GENERAL LAND OFFICE by the SURVEYOR GENERAL, which said Tract has been purchased by the said

Now know ye, That the **United States of America,** in consideration of the premises, and in conformity with the several Acts of Congress in such case made and provided, Have given and granted, and by these presents **Do give and grant,** unto the said William H. Hardy _____

_____ heirs, the said Tract above described: **To have and to hold** the same, together with all the rights, privileges, immunities, and appurtenances, of whatsoever nature, thereunto belonging, unto the said William H. Hardy _____ and to his _____ heirs and assigns forever.

In testimony whereof, I, Chester A. Arthur _____ . President of the United States of America, have caused these letters to be made Patent, and the seal of the GENERAL LAND OFFICE to be hereunto affixed.

Given under my hand, at the CITY OF WASHINGTON, the tenth day of May , in the year of our Lord one thousand eight hundred and eighty-two , and of the Independence of the United States the one hundred and eighth .

By the President: Chester A. Arthur

By _____ , Secretary.

RECORDED, Vol. _____ , Page _____ . _____ , Recorder of the General Land Office.

This land grant to William H. Hardy, dated May 10, 1882, details the purchase of "the east half of the northwest quarter and the southwest quarter of the northwest quarter of section eleven in township five north of range thirteen west of St. Stephens Meridian in Mississippi, containing one hundred and nineteen acres and seventy-six hundredths of an acre" from the General Land Office in Jackson, Mississippi. Hardy used the acreage to found the city he had dreamed of two years earlier on the banks of Gordon Creek. The settlement, formerly called Gordonville, was renamed Hattiesburg in honor of his second wife, Hattie. (Photograph courtesy of the University of Southern Mississippi McCain Library & Archives.)

William Harris Hardy posed for his Mississippi Bar Association photograph in 1903. He retired as president of the Gulf & Ship Island Railroad Company when he was elected to the Mississippi State Senate in 1895. During his term in the state senate, Hardy chaired both the Committee on Corporations and the Finance Committee and introduced a bill to remove the penitentiary from Jackson (it was relocated to Parchman Farm in 1901) and build a new capitol on the site. He served as a judge from 1905 until 1909. For the remaining eight years of his life, he returned to work as a lawyer in a Gulfport firm he had started with his son Toney. (Photograph courtesy of the University of Southern Mississippi McCain Library & Archives.)

Above, William H. Hardy is seen with Mr. amd Mrs. Thomas Hardy. Below, W.H. celebrates his 80th birthday on February 12, 1917, surrounded by members of his family at his Gulfport home. Five days later, his death would be mourned across the state. Pictured are, from left to right, (first row) Ida Hardy (W.H. Hardy's third wife), W.H. Hardy, Mattie Hardy Lott, and an unidentified son of Ida and W.H. Hardy; (second row) Mabel Hardy, Lizzie Hardy Huey, Jeff D. Hardy with an unidentified child, and Lamar Hardy; (third row) Edwin Huey, Blanche Hardy, Toney Hardy, and Lena Mai Hardy McDonald. (Photographs courtesy of the University of Southern Mississippi McCain Library & Archives.)

Pictured left is a bust of W.H. Hardy covered with an American flag prior to its unveiling. In addition to founding Hattiesburg and Laurel, William H. Hardy also went on to found the city of Gulfport, Mississippi, where he retired and was buried. Twin busts of Hardy were unveiled in Gulfport and Hattiesburg shortly after his death on February 17, 1917. Note the wreaths commemorating his excellence and service to his community on the unveiled bust, seen below. The bust's inscription lists Hardy's many roles and accomplishments and calls him "a dreamer, whose dreams came true." (Photographs courtesy of the University of Southern Mississippi McCain Library & Archives.)

WILLIAM HARRIS HARDY
BORN LOWNDES CO. ALA.
FEB. 12, 1837
DIED GULFPORT, MISS.
FEB. 19, 1917
FOUNDER OF THE CITIES OF
GULFPORT
AND
HATTIESBURG

William Harris Hardy was laid to rest at the Evergreen Cemetery in Gulfport, Mississippi. The *Hattiesburg American* commemorated his "proud and independent spirit . . . [and his] vision of development which smiles from South Mississippi today in many a field, hums in many a mill, rattles in many a rail and car, and swells in the voices of a great and progressive population." (Photograph courtesy of the University of Southern Mississippi McCain Library & Archives.)

WILLIAM HARRIS HARDY

In 1880 near the banks of Gordon Creek, this lawyer, railroad builder and Confederate veteran selected the site for Hattiesburg. Incorporated in 1884, the town was named for Hardy's wife, Hattie Lott.

This marker describing the 1880s founding of the "Hub City" is on West Pine Street in downtown Hattiesburg. Erected in 1974 by the Hattiesburg Historical Society, it is roughly 400 feet away from a bust of Hardy, which stands on West Front Street. (Photograph courtesy of the University of Southern Mississippi McCain Library & Archives.)

Two

RAILS AND LUMBER

The name Forrest, if seen as nothing more than a coincidental homophone, still conjures those great bygone forests to which the county owes its very existence. After the Choctaws were displaced by the Treaty of Mount Dexter of 1805, new white settlers needed timber to construct houses and barns and also wanted clear-cut pastures. After the completion of railroads connecting the region to the Mississippi Gulf Coast, New Orleans, Natchez, Jackson, Meridian, and Mobile, the lumber industry was set to oblige farmers' wishes for pastureland with ruthless efficiency, paying them next to nothing (as little as $1.25 an acre) to harvest trees that were centuries old.

Longleaf yellow pine, a popular general structural material, was second only in strength and longevity to cypress. During the heyday of the South Mississippi lumber boom, longleaf pine was prized throughout Europe, South America, South Africa, and the Caribbean.

From 1908 to 1915, Mississippi ranked third in the United States for lumber production, and longleaf pine manufactured in the southern part of the state constituted about 80 percent of the state's total output. Hattiesburg and Laurel were noted as the two most important lumber centers east of the Mississippi River. At this time, sawmills were the major employers in Forrest County, and the workforce (white and black) was drawn from men working on unproductive farms in the surrounding area. This led to a shift in the population from the country to the sawmill town. Laborers earned, on average, 10¢ an hour and worked 11 hours a day, six days a week. Though the workforce was segregated, with white men holding all the key jobs, if a man had the ability, he could often get and hold a sawmill job regardless of his ethnicity.

The impact the railroads and lumber industry had on this region cannot be emphasized enough. In 1899, when Gov. A.J. McLaurin proclaimed Hattiesburg a city, the population was 3,600. The city's population would nearly quadruple in a decade; by 1910, Forrest County was home to 20,772 residents, and the population of Hattiesburg alone had risen to 11,773.

Loggers Monroe Lott (left) and Everett Lott use a crosscut saw to fell a mighty longleaf pine for the J.J. Newman Lumber Company. A log from this virgin pine, which was probably more than a century old, won a steam locomotive as a prize at the 1904 World's Fair in St. Louis, Missouri. (Photograph courtesy of the University of Southern Mississippi McCain Library & Archives.)

Four unidentified loggers stand by a yellow pine in the early 1900s. Before the 1880s, loggers used axes to cut down trees. The use of the two-man crosscut saw drastically improved the efficiency of lumber harvests. These men worked for Walworth & Neville Manufacturing, located in the Pinebur area, about 40 miles east-southeast of Hattiesburg. This tree was likely fashioned into a telephone pole crossarm. (Photograph courtesy of the University of Southern Mississippi McCain Library & Archives.)

Turpentine extraction was one of the Hattiesburg area's earliest industries. Turpentine was derived from the resin of pine trees. After the bark was removed, workers would hack V-shaped marks (called "catfaces" for their resemblance to the whiskers of a cat) into the pines. A bucket was affixed below the marks to collect the resin that the tree produced to seal the surface of the wound. After the resin was collected, it was distilled in copper stills. (Photograph courtesy of the University of Southern Mississippi McCain Library & Archives.)

Before the railroad revolutionized the logging industry in South Mississippi, lumbermen required ox-powered wagons and hard labor to transport lumber from the virgin pine forests. These pictures, from around the early 1900s, depict the labor-intensive task of moving the mighty longleaf pines from the forests to the mills. (Photographs courtesy of the University of Southern Mississippi McCain Library & Archives.)

In 1880, before railroads were operating at full steam, there were less than 300 sawmills in Mississippi. By the close of the century, after substantial tracks had been laid, Mississippi had well over 600 mills that were generating over a billion board feet of lumber annually. This output would continue to skyrocket; by 1915, a number of sawmills were each generating more than 30,000 board feet of lumber per day (close to 10 million board feet annually). From 1908 to 1915, Mississippi ranked third in the United States in lumber production, behind Washington and Louisiana. (Photographs courtesy of the University of Southern Mississippi McCain Library & Archives.)

A 50-ton Heisler steam engine pulls lumber across the South Mississippi countryside in July 1928, destined to replace decking on the famed USS *Constitution*. The battleship, affectionately called "Old Ironsides," was launched in 1797 and is the world's oldest naval vessel still afloat. The lumber was processed at the Major-Sowers sawmill Tallahala site in Perry County, about 12 miles from Hattiesburg. (Photograph courtesy of the University of Southern Mississippi McCain Library & Archives.)

The Tatum Company No. 2, a 30-ton Lima steam engine with a 2-6-0 configuration, is parked in front of a barn. (Photographs courtesy of the University of Southern Mississippi McCain Library & Archives.)

The Southern Railway Company constructed its Hattiesburg depot in 1910. The Italian Renaissance–style structure was designed by well-known architect Frank P. Milburn to reflect the people of Hattiesburg's grand vision of their city's future and has been in continuous use since its construction. In 2000, the City of Hattiesburg bought the depot and the surrounding 3.2 acres and initiated a $10 million, seven-year restoration project, which was overseen by Albert & Associates Architects and completed in 2007. Located in downtown Hattiesburg, the 14,900-square-foot depot is capped by a clay-tiled roof and includes a 4,000-square-foot passenger waiting area. (Photograph courtesy of Brooke Cruthirds.)

Passengers load onto a Mississippi Central Railroad train at the Sumrall Depot in the early 1900s. The depot was built in 1907. (Photograph courtesy of the University of Southern Mississippi McCain Library & Archives.)

In 1923, W.S.F. Tatum (owner of Tatum Lumber Company and primary benefactor of William Carey University) founded the Bonhomie & Hattiesburg Southern Railway Company (B&HS), establishing a line from Hattiesburg to Beaumont. By connecting to the Gulf, Mobile & Ohio Railroad in Beaumont, the Tatum Lumber Company connected vast tracts of timberland to the sawmill in Bonhomie. The B&HS No. 300 was built in February 1925 by Baldwin Locomotive Works and saw continuous service until its retirement in 1961. This locomotive had a steam-and-coal-driven engine and a "Mikado" (2-8-2) wheel arrangement (two leading wheels on one axle followed by eight driving wheels on four axles followed by two trailing wheels on one axle) and cost $28,500 brand new. Presently, it is on display in downtown Hattiesburg. (Photographs courtesy of the University of Southern Mississippi McCain Library & Archives.)

Bonhomie & Hattiesburg Southern No. 200 was built in March 1925—just a month after B&HS No. 300 was completed—by Baldwin Locomotive Works. The locomotive had an "American" (4-4-0) wheel arrangement (four leading wheels on two axles followed by four coupled and powered driving wheels and no trailing wheels) and cost $19,285 brand-new. In 1953, B&HS was sold, and this coal-and-steam-powered juggernaut was scrapped and replaced by a diesel EMD-SM1 engine capable of producing 600 horsepower. Today, the former B&HS railway line is used by Canadian National as part of a network that chiefly transports coal between Jackson and Mobile. (Photographs courtesy of the University of Southern Mississippi McCain Library & Archives.)

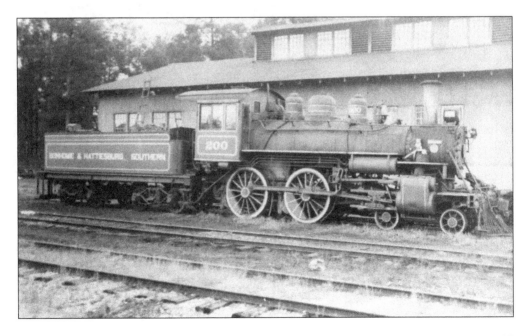

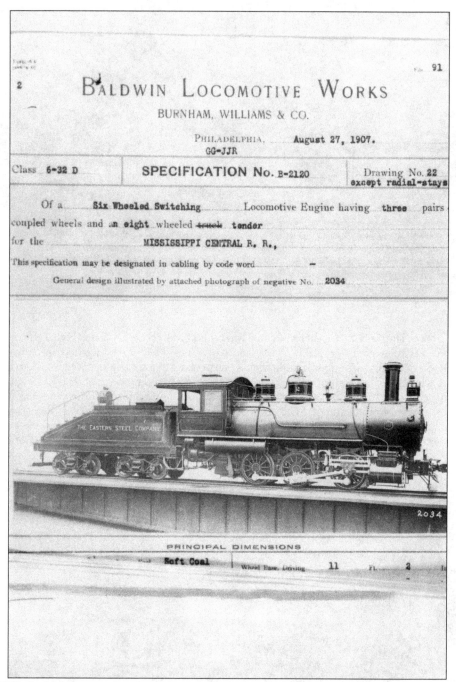

BALDWIN LOCOMOTIVE WORKS

BURNHAM, WILLIAMS & CO.

PHILADELPHIA, **August 27, 1907.**
GG-JJR

| Class **6-32 D** | SPECIFICATION No. **B-2120** | Drawing No. **22** except **radial-stays** |

Of a **Six Wheeled Switching** Locomotive Engine having **three** pairs coupled wheels and **an eight** wheeled ~~truck~~ **tender**

for the **MISSISSIPPI CENTRAL R. R.,**

This specification may be designated in cabling by code word

General design illustrated by attached photograph of negative No. **2034**

THE EASTERN STEEL COMPANY

2034

PRINCIPAL DIMENSIONS

Soft Coal | Wheel Base, Driving **11** Ft. **2**

In 1897, the J.J. Newman Lumber Company built the Pearl & Leaf Rivers Railroad connecting Hattiesburg to Sumrall. The name was change in 1904 to the Mississippi Central Railroad, and the railway continued to creep east, reaching Natchez by the 1920s. This 1907 specification sheet for Baldwin Locomotive Works notes a "six wheeled switching locomotive" ordered by Mississippi Central Railroad. This heavy engine, designed to produce massive amounts of torque, was primarily used as a workhorse, disassembling and assembling trains as they come into the train yard. (Photograph courtesy of the University of Southern Mississippi McCain Library & Archives.)

The Gulf & Ship Island Railroad (G&SI) was one of Hattiesburg's greatest post–Civil War benefactors. Though its total economic impact on the state of Mississippi might be immeasurable, the benefits of establishing a railroad that connected a state still reeling from the Civil War were both immediate and apparent. The G&SI allowed lumber interests to operate in previously inaccessible areas and provided a means for companies to deliver their good to worldwide markets. Company towns sprouted up, sometimes before the tracks were even completed. The company operated exclusively in the state of Mississippi and owned approximately 160 miles of standard-gauge main rail line, 150 miles of branch lines, and over 100 miles of track in Gulfport. (Photograph courtesy of the University of Southern Mississippi McCain Library & Archives.)

Tatum Lumber Company Train No. 5, seen here at the Bonhomie Sawmill, was built in 1919 and weighed about 60 tons. The lumber and railroad industries enjoyed a happy and profitable marriage in South Mississippi, and neither would have developed here without the other. (Photograph courtesy of the University of Southern Mississippi McCain Library & Archives.)

Three

INDUSTRY AND GROWTH

Hattiesburg, which had benefited greatly during its first three decades from the establishment of Camp Shelby and its two universities, continued its romance with technology (initiated by the railroads that now crisscrossed at the city's heart) by welcoming innovation and industry. These developments included the Hercules plant, built by DuPont in 1926; Saenger Theater, which boasted the first public air-conditioning in the state (a remarkable milestone for anyone who has spent a summer in South Mississippi); Reliance Manufacturing Company, which began producing garments downtown in 1933; Merchant's Grocery Company, established in Hattiesburg in 1904 and now a national wholesale food distributor and restaurant supplier under the name of Merchants Foodservice; the H.C. Hudson Company, which invented the fire sale in 1938 and founded Hudson Incorporated, one of the largest retailers of salvage goods in the nation; and Forrest General Hospital, opened in 1952 and currently second only to Camp Shelby as Hattiesburg's largest employer.

While it should come as no surprise the people of South Mississippi have proudly held dear to their traditions, it is refreshing to note the innovative spirit that possessed many of Hattiesburg's businessmen at the beginning of the 19th century. Electricity was coursing through power lines newly strung between poles manufactured by nearby mills out of local yellow pines. Stuart C. Irby, a particularly forward-thinking businessman who presided over the Commerce Department of the Hattiesburg Traction Company (Hattiesburg Trolley System) beginning in 1913, advocated the wondrous possibilities electricity promised by converting one of Hattiesburg's five trolley cars into a moveable demonstration booth. Irby likened the promotional campaign to "taking the mountain to Mahomet"—saying that while "Mahomet found it easier to go the mountain than to make the mountain come to him" the Hattiesburg Traction company found it easier to take the colorfully decorated demonstration trolley car, equipped with phonographs, toasters, laundry machines, and other electrical devices, to the customers. The trolley car elicited the attention of hundreds of residents who were intrigued by the newfangled contraptions, and it became a unique cultural event that helped usher the city of Hattiesburg into the age of modern conveniences.

An early-1900s view of Main Street in downtown Hattiesburg shows the Bufkin & Cadenhead
Drugstore (left). The eye-catching building was constructed in 1905 and was restored in 1989 by
Albert & Associates Architects. A horse and buggy is parked on Main Street, in front of the store.
(Photograph courtesy of the University of Southern Mississippi McCain Library & Archives.)

Uniformed trolley conductors line up on the tracks in front of trolley cars. Also pictured are three children and three men in civilian clothing. The Hattiesburg Traction Company ran 12 electric-powered trolley cars, one trailer, and three work cars in its heyday—the early 1900s until 1925, when the trolley cars were replaced with buses. Car No. 109 is seen to the left, behind the conductors. (Photograph courtesy of the University of Southern Mississippi McCain Library & Archives.)

This 1920s view of downtown Hattiesburg's South Main Street shows an electric trolley car riding along the tracks. A broken-down, early-model work truck is seen to the right, just across the short wooden bridge. Power lines—the poles and crossarms of which were likely manufactured out of yellow pines from the area—line the sides of the busy street. (Photograph courtesy of the University of Southern Mississippi McCain Library & Archives.)

The Aladdin Company manufactured prefabricated houses, which were extremely popular in boomtowns like Hattiesburg in the early 1900s. Prefabricated houses were relatively inexpensive and could be erected in a day—factors which undoubtedly met the primary requirements of the throngs of workers flocking to Hattiesburg. The company's diverse workforce—black and white, male and female—is pictured outside the company building located at the intersection of North Street and the Mississippi Central Railroad track. (Photograph courtesy of the University of Southern Mississippi McCain Library & Archives.)

Hattiesburg was in no short supply of lumber, as evidenced by the piles pictured here in front of a row of newly constructed houses along Bay Street sometime between 1905 and 1915. Most of these early homes still stand today, and a number of them have been fully restored by their individual owners. (Photograph courtesy of the University of Southern Mississippi McCain Library & Archives.)

COMPLIMENTS *of*
PEOPLES BANK

PEOPLES BANK

PEOPLE'S
BANK
CAPITAL $10,000.00

HATTIESBURG,
MISS.

Despite the evils of segregation, the Mobile-Bouie area was a vibrant aggregation of black-owned businesses—a town unto itself, complete with grocery stores, movie theaters, photographers, mechanics, and more. The People's Bank, located on Mobile Street, was owned and operated by E.D. Howell, a prominent member of the community. (Photograph courtesy of the Deborah Denard Delgado family.)

Above, this extraordinarily rare photograph, from around 1900, shows Ed Howell driving a horse-drawn carriage on Fifth Street. In addition to founding the People's Bank, Howell also owned a local furniture store. At left, this *New York Times* newspaper article describes the March 19, 1907, assassination of Ed Howell. As the article states, the shooting is a mystery. At the time of his murder, Howell had retired as president of the bank and was working as the institution's cashier. The new president of the bank, Joseph Pettus, and the vice president, Joseph Williams, were both implicated in Howell's death. It was alleged that Howell was killed because he had the combination to the bank's safe—$2,700 in cash was discovered missing after his murder. Pettus and Williams were tried for grand larceny and Howell's murder multiple times but were never convicted. (Above, photograph courtesy of the Deborah Denard Delgado family; left, courtesy of the *New York Times*.)

The Ross Sanatorium was established as Hattiesburg's first hospital in 1900 under the supervision of T.E. Ross, one of the driving forces behind the founding of Mississippi Normal College (which later became the University of Southern Mississippi). The hospital quickly outgrew its original facilities and moved to a new location at Hall Avenue and Bay Street (above), where it was renamed the Gulf & Ship Island Railroad Employees Hospital in 1903. The G&SI Hospital became the Methodist Hospital (below) in 1921 and underwent several transformations throughout the 20th century. Its most current incarnation is the Wesley Medical Center, located on US Highway 98 in West Hattiesburg. (Photographs courtesy of the University of Southern Mississippi McCain Library & Archives.)

SOUTH MISSISSIPPI INFIRMARY, HATTIESBURG, MISS.

Above, this 1905 photograph shows the front of the South Mississippi Infirmary on Walnut Street. The facility was owned and operated by Dr. Walter Wesley Crawford, a very prominent and influential physician who was perhaps most noted for his role in attracting the establishment of Camp Shelby in the Hattiesburg area. Below, the South Mississippi Infirmary can be seen to the right of the Crawford home and grounds. Dr. Crawford's home still stands, maintained by his descendants. (Photographs courtesy of the University of Southern Mississippi McCain Library & Archives.)

Barron Motor Works, the local Lincoln, Ford, and Fordson (Ford's tractor division from 1917 to 1964) dealer was located in downtown Hattiesburg in a large brick building at the corner of Main and Batson Streets. Above, Barron Motor Works employees pose in front of the building behind early-model Fords in a 1920s photograph. Down the street, a horse and buggy can be faintly seen. Below, an alternate perspective of the building affords a view of Batson Street. The company was dissolved in 1928, and since 1986 the lot has been occupied by the Paul B. Johnson Jr. Chancery Court Building. (Photographs courtesy of the University of Southern Mississippi McCain Library & Archives.)

Before being converted into a Sinclair service station in 1933, the building above (located downtown at the corner of Eaton and Forrest Streets) housed the Hulett Undertaking Company. This photograph was taken before Sinclair Oil adopted a brontosaurus as its logo. The new logo would be spawned by an exhibit at the 1933–1934 World's Fair in Chicago designed to show the relation between dinosaurs and fossil fuels, which had as its centerpiece a two-ton rubber replica of a brontosaurus. Below, in this interior view of the H.E. Bro Auto Accessory Store located on East Pine Street, are, from left to right, Stanford Gunn Sr., Lamar Bro, Eli Bro, and Peter Bro. An unidentified employee can also be seen, peeking out of a back room. (Photographs courtesy of the University of Southern Mississippi McCain Library & Archives.)

Above, this 1926 photograph shows one-stop shopping on downtown Hattiesburg's North Main Street. Businesses include, from left to right, an American Oil Company service station, Owl Drugs, and a Piggly Wiggly grocery store. Below, the Hattiesburg Bottling Company on Mobile Street was built in 1915 and boasted Hattiesburg's first elevator. This 1920 photograph tells of the changing times. Note the mix of horse-drawn carriages and automobiles parked on the street outside the two-story building. The plant shut down in 1960, and the building remained vacant until being remodeled in 2004 as a restaurant and music venue. (Photographs courtesy of the University of Southern Mississippi McCain Library & Archives.)

Smith's Drugstore on Mobile Street was owned and operated by Hammond Smith from 1925 until his retirement in 1980. Smith, a prominent Hattiesburg businessman for over half a century, was also one of the city's first registered black voters. Pictured here are some of the most prominent businessmen of the Mobile-Bouie area in the 1920s. They are, from left to right, (front row) Dr. Martin Luther Smith (Hammond's brother), Albert White, Dr. Tally, unidentified "reverend," and D.W. White Sr.; (back row) E. Hammond Smith, Principal Adkinson, unidentified "reverend," Buck McClendon, Reverend Perkins, unidentified, and Mike "the barber." (Photograph courtesy of the Deborah Denard Delgado family.)

Employees stand outside the Phoenix Laundry & Dry Cleaners in this early-1900s photograph. The company, which opened before the turn of the century, offered a pickup-and-delivery service using the horse-drawn carriages seen outside the building. (Photograph courtesy of the University of Southern Mississippi McCain Library & Archives.)

Above, the first manned flight in Hattiesburg took place at Camp Shelby in 1917. This hallmark event sparked a slew of air shows over the next few years, including exhibitions from famed female aviator Ruth Law. According to World War I–era letters, "Ruth Law gave an exhibition on the 27th in her one passenger aeroplane. The boys had to hand it to her for the daredevil stuff. She made two flights and looped the loop about 1,500 feet above the ground." Below, the Hattiesburg-Bobby L. Chain Municipal Airport has provided air service to the area since opening in 1930. During World War II, it was one of a number of civilian airports leased and updated by the US Army Air Corps. The update to the facility included concrete runways, seen in this image from between around 1939 and 1945, as well as new airplane hangars, taxiways, and a control tower. (Photographs courtesy of the University of Southern Mississippi McCain Library & Archives.)

Above, before building a Hattiesburg plant in 1920, California Powder Works renamed itself Hercules to emphasize the potency of the explosive black powder it produced. This aerial view shows the scope of the Hercules Powder Company Plant on West Seventh Street, near the Mobile-Bouie neighborhood in downtown Hattiesburg. Hercules began operations at its 168-acre facility in 1923 and produced over 250 varieties of chemicals until shutting down in 2009. In 2011, the Environmental Protection Agency deemed that soil surrounding the plant and several water supplies (including Green's Creek and the Bouie River) were contaminated and ordered continual monitoring and testing to assess the potential hazards posed by the plant's operations. Mobile-Bouie historians claim it was common for community members to dip their dogs and cats into the Hercules Plant drainage ditches to rid them of fleas and ticks. Below, this interior view of an unidentified mill dates to around the 1920s. (Photographs courtesy of the University of Southern Mississippi McCain Library & Archives.)

Ready to serve, employees stand behind the counters of the H.G. Hill grocery store on West Pine Street in 1932. The company, based out of Nashville, Tennessee, enjoyed its fair measure of success and opened a Super Food Market on Hardy Street in 1947. (Photograph courtesy of the University of Southern Mississippi McCain Library & Archives.)

Employees stand for a picture outside the Hattiesburg warehouse of the Merchant's Company Grocers in the 1920s. Now a national wholesale food distributor and restaurant supplier (Merchants Foodservice), the Merchant's Grocery Company was founded in Hattiesburg in 1904 and began construction on this two-story warehouse in 1907. The company, which by 1923 was generating $1 million annually, quickly expanded operations to Laurel and Jackson. Today, the company's distribution network covers nine states in the southeastern United States. (Photograph courtesy of the University of Southern Mississippi McCain Library & Archives.)

In this 1920s photograph, men work at their desks in the Komp Equipment Company offices on East Pine Street in Hattiesburg. The Hattiesburg Machinery & Car Manufacturing Company was established in 1889 by George Komp, who arrived in town with $1,000 to his name. The company prospered under Komp's direction, and he renamed it Komp Machine Works in 1901 after buying all outstanding stock. The company has endured for over a century, manufacturing a variety of products, including parts for lumber mills at the beginning of the 20th century and ammunition during World War II. Today, the company manufactures welding supplies. (Photograph courtesy of the University of Southern Mississippi McCain Library & Archives.)

Four

EDUCATIONAL INSTITUTIONS

Hattiesburg experienced exponential growth during the first few decades of the 20th century, a period that saw the genesis of its two universities. Significantly, both universities were built on land donated by lumber interests. William Carey was founded on property donated by Willie Sion Franklin Tatum, founder of the Tatum Lumber Company, that consisted of two surviving frame buildings left over from lumber operations and 10 acres of cutover land. The University of Southern Mississippi was founded on 120 acres that, according to the original deed to the USM campus, was sold to the trustees "of the State Normal College of the State of Mississippi" for "One Dollar in hand paid" by A.A. Montague, T.E. Ross, and Herbert A. Camp of the Camp & Hinton Brothers Lumber Company.

William Carey University began in Poplarville, Mississippi, as the Pearl River Boarding School in 1892. The school was consumed by fire in 1905. Unable to secure funding to rebuild in Poplarville, school founder W.I. Thames moved to Hattiesburg and secured enough financial backing to open South Mississippi College in 1906. Tragically, fire also destroyed most of that school 1910. Willie Sion Franklin Tatum bought the land and donated it to the Mississippi Baptist Convention with the stipulations that the school operate as a Christian school for women for five years and that at least 100 students be enrolled during the first year. Mississippi Woman's College successfully fulfilled Tatum's requests from 1911 to 1940, when it was forced to close due to Depression-era economic woes. The grounds were used from 1940 to 1946 to house Army officers based at Camp Shelby, and in 1946, the school reopened and operated as it had before (strictly admitting only women) until the Mississippi Baptist Convention voted to change to a coeducational school in 1953. In 1954, the school was renamed William Carey College, and in 2006 it was renamed again to William Carey University, reflecting its new accreditation status with the Southern Association of Colleges and Schools.

Mississippi Normal College was founded in 1910 as Mississippi's first state-supported teachers' training school. The school was originally encompassed five buildings, including the principal academic building, separate men's and women's dormitories, the Industrial Cottage devoted to sewing and cooking instruction, and the President's Home. In 1922, Mississippi Normal College granted its first baccalaureate degree. In 1924, the school's name was changed to the State Teachers College, and in 1940 it was changed again to Mississippi Southern College. In 1942, the US War Department added an administration-training school to the campus to train staff for World War II military camps. African American Clyde Kennard tried repeatedly—in 1956, 1957, and 1959—to enroll in the still-segregated school. Kennard would ultimately die of intestinal cancer three years into a seven-year sentence at Parchment Prison after being framed for stealing chicken feed. The school was renamed the University of Southern Mississippi in 1962, and later that year, it awarded its first doctoral degree. In 1965, the first black students, Raylawni Young Branch and Gwendolyn Elaine Armstrong, were admitted.

Mississippi Normal College counted 227 students and 17 faculty members during its first term in 1912, and 876 students were enrolled for the first summer session from June 9, 1913, to July 18, 1913. This panoramic view includes the entire faculty and student body. The five original buildings of the campus can be seen in the background. To the left, in front, is College Hall, the main academic building, which housed classrooms, administrative offices, the library, and

HATTIESBURG AND MISSISSIPPI HALLS

This 1925 picture shows both women's residence halls on the campus of the newly renamed State Teachers College. Hattiesburg Hall, built in 1912 to serve as the women's dormitory, now serves as a dormitory for male students who maintain a certain grade point average. Mississippi Hall, built in 1914, now serves as a dormitory for female students who maintain a good GPA. Today, the University of Southern Mississippi has a dozen residence halls in addition to a new residence complex built specifically for sororities and female athletes and an on-campus apartment complex that houses graduate students and undergraduates with families. (Photograph courtesy of the University of Southern Mississippi McCain Library & Archives.)

an auditorium; behind it is Forrest County Hall, the men's dormitory, and to the right of Forrest County Hall is Hattiesburg Hall, the identical women's dormitory. The Industrial Cottage (now the Honor House) and the President's Home (now the Ogletree House) can be found to the far right (the view of the President's Home is partially blocked by a pine tree). (Photograph courtesy of the University of Southern Mississippi McCain Library & Archives.)

Chinaberry trees planted by Joseph Anderson Cook, the first president of Mississippi Normal College (now the University of Southern Mississippi), line a road on campus in this 1920s photograph. The school was founded in 1910 on 120 acres of cutover timberland. Today, the university's Hattiesburg campus encompasses over 300 acres and includes 180 buildings. (Photograph courtesy of the University of Southern Mississippi McCain Library & Archives.)

Mississippi Normal College received the authority to confer baccalaureate degrees in 1922, and it continued to expand in terms of faculty and staff, being renamed State Teachers College in 1924. The school offered full tuition waivers to graduates who promised to teach in the state's public schools for a time equal to what they spent at the college. Otherwise, the total estimated expenses—including tuition, housing, food, medical and travel expenses, and incidentals—amounted to less than $300 for nine months. The school promised a clean, wholesome environment that encouraged students to take special interest in bettering their communities. To that end, the institution promoted, according to the college's 1927 bulletin, "every form of wholesome organized sports." These pictures of the school's women's formal gymnastics appear in the yearbook, *Neka Camon* (meaning "the new spirit"). (Photographs courtesy of the University of Southern Mississippi McCain Library & Archives.)

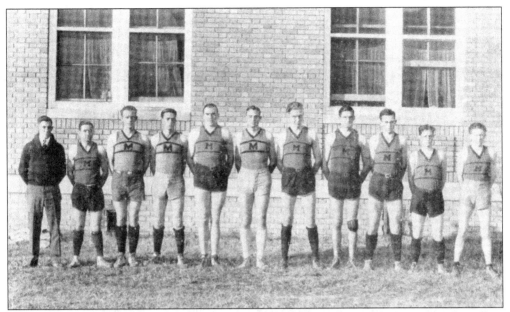

Pictured here is the 1926 State Teachers College varsity basketball team. In 1912, when the college (then named Mississippi Normal College) opened, over 150 students formed an athletic association under the direction of science instructor Ronald J. Slay. The college's basketball team began with an undefeated (3-0) season in 1912–1913. According to some, the school began offering four-year baccalaureate degrees to attract and retain better players for its athletic programs. Fred "Tiny" Davis (great-grandfather of author Colter Cruthirds) is standing fifth from the left. (Photograph courtesy of the University of Southern Mississippi McCain Library & Archives.)

The school's dining hall, one of the most important buildings on campus, is pictured here around 1925, not long after a state legislative act on March 7, 1924, changed the institution's name to State Teachers College. Note that many of the women are toting parasols on this sunny day. The original dining hall has long since been razed, and the area is now the location of Danforth Chapel. (Photograph courtesy of the University of Southern Mississippi McCain Library & Archives.)

The college's football program, like its basketball program, began in 1912. The inaugural game was played at Kamper Park, a mile away from the campus, and the Mississippi Normal College football team won 30-0. The team would continue to play at Kamper Park until 1932—excepting the 1917 and 1918 seasons, when the athletic programs were suspended in favor of focus on the war effort. The 1926 Yellow Jackets are pictured here. Fred "Tiny" Davis, voted the school's "best all-around athlete" in 1929, can be seen at the center of the top row in the above photograph and third from left in the top row of the photograph below. (Photographs courtesy of the University of Southern Mississippi McCain Library & Archives.)

Built in 1932, the powerhouse at the Mississippi Teachers College contained three levels of gas boilers and had a 100-foot-tall smokestack. It served as a heating hub for other buildings on campus. Unused for decades, it has since been renovated to house the Powerhouse Restaurant. The area in the foreground of the image is now occupied by Cook Library. (Photograph courtesy of the University of Southern Mississippi McCain Library & Archives.)

Built in 1912, College Hall was one of the five original buildings on campus. It was the principal academic building, housing classrooms, administrative offices, the school library, and an auditorium. The auditorium (pictured here) was located on the third floor and featured a mural that depicted a narrative of what the college could offer the surrounding area: the image moves from a rustic cabin in the woods to a clear-cut field with students filing into a schoolhouse. (Photograph courtesy of the University of Southern Mississippi McCain Library & Archives.)

Initiated as a campus beautification project by Claude Bennett, the institution's second president, the Sunken Garden was completed by student efforts between 1929 and 1932. North of the gardens is the President's Home (now the Ogletree House), one of the oldest buildings on campus. The Sunken Garden has long been filled in and, since 1956, has been the site of McLemore Hall. (Photograph courtesy of the University of Southern Mississippi McCain Library & Archives.)

Above, the king and queen and their court, wearing elaborate costumes for the Spring Festival at Mississippi Woman's College (now William Carey University), gather around a pond in this 1930s image. As the name suggests, Mississippi Woman's College was an all-female school, and there were no male kings in this court. Below, several young ladies in costume dance around the maypole. (Photographs courtesy of the University of Southern Mississippi McCain Library & Archives.)

Willie Sion Franklin Tatum, a lumber magnate, donated the property for the school with the stipulation that the institution operate as a Christian school for women for five years and that at least 100 students be enrolled the first year. Throughout his life, Tatum used his power and wealth to promote Christianity. For instance, he had a general policy that his sawmills and even his railroads not operate on Sundays (except in extreme emergencies) so that his workers could attend church. (Photograph courtesy of William Carey University.)

Tatum Court, the administration building of Mississippi Woman's College was built in 1914 and named for the college's most influential early benefactor. (Photograph courtesy of William Carey University.)

Above, built in 1919, Ross and Johnson Halls (right) were among the first buildings on the then 10-acre campus of the Mississippi Woman's College. The brick structures served as dormitories, and a covered walkway offered residents easy access to the dining hall, seen to the left. Below, the one-story brick building housed the Mary Ross Memorial Hospital after its completion in 1923. It presently houses faculty offices and conference rooms for the School of Business. (Photographs courtesy of William Carey University.)

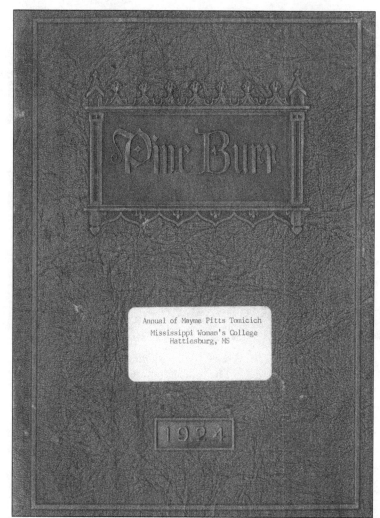

The *Pine Burr* was published annually by the students and faculty of Mississippi Woman's College from 1913 to 1955. The institution became the coeducational William Carey University in 1954, and in 1956 the annual publication was renamed the *Crusader*. (Photograph courtesy of the University of Southern Mississippi McCain Library & Archives.)

Annual of Mayme Pitts Tomicich
Mississippi Woman's College
Hattiesburg, MS

1924

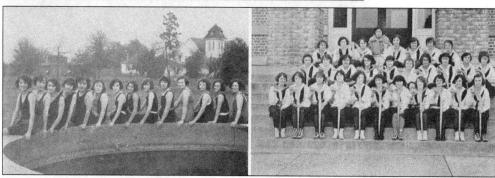

The 1924 *Pine Burr* shows that year's swimming and field hockey teams. The *Pine Burr* notes that it was the college's credo to develop "all-round girls, both physically and mentally" and proposes that "swimming is one of the best forms of outdoor sports to develop and build up our physiques." As for field hockey, the annual hyped the growing popularity of the sport, saying, "the supposition is that in time, hockey will replace all other games for women." (Photograph courtesy of the University of Southern Mississippi McCain Library & Archives.)

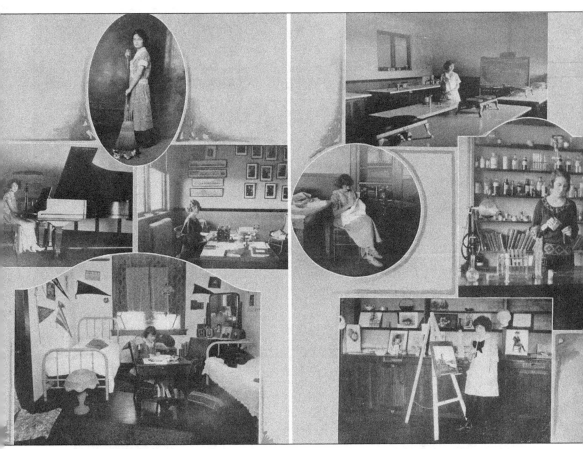

These pages from the 1924 *Pine Burr* indicate some of the curriculum designed to sculpt an all-around Christian lady of the time and are captioned "At Work." On the left page, Johnnie Benson is seen sweeping, Kathleen Sanders is playing the piano, Ruby Francis is typing, and Valeria Morgan is diligently studying in her dormitory room. The right page shows Mamye Griffis cooking, Gladys Bell sewing, Mattie Laura McKinnon working in the chemistry lab, and Marie Magee painting in the art studio. (Photograph courtesy of the University of Southern Mississippi McCain Library & Archives.)

This spread from the 1924 *Pine Burr* is captioned "At Play." The images on the left page include a view of Ruby Caperton, Floretta Wright, Helen Hanna, and Helen Polk in the campus tea garden; May Jones and Marguerite Blankenship exhibiting all their female wiles at a dinner; Ruth Polk readying to leave for a party; and Mary Pryor, Edith Odom, Louise Clower, Minnie Walton, and Doly Hardin providing after-dinner entertainment. On the right page, Odelle Sarphie is ready for a drive (top); Julia Toy Johnson is ready to fish (left); Dixie Simmons is swinging a golf club (right); and Sama Phillips, Ada Mae Landrum, Mary Louise Hays, Tinye Belle Odom, and Annie Kate White sit down for a feast (bottom). (Photograph courtesy of the University of Southern Mississippi McCain Library & Archives.)

This North Main Street building was constructed in 1911 to house Hattiesburg High School and was substantially enlarged during a second phase of construction, completed 10 years later. It served as the high school until 1959 and then as an administration building for the Hattiesburg Public School System until the 1980s, when it was transformed into an antiques mall. It sustained damage in 2005 as a result of Hurricane Katrina and in 2007 from arson. The Mississippi Heritage Trust lists the Old Hattiesburg High School as one of the 10 most endangered Mississippi landmarks, largely because it is one of the few examples of Jacobethan architecture in Mississippi. (Photograph courtesy of Brooke Cruthirds.)

This 1902 view of Hattiesburg's black schoolhouse precipitated the need for a modern school building within the community. This class photograph, with students lined up outside the front door of their one-room schoolhouse, is the only view of this structure known to exist. (Photograph courtesy of the University of Southern Mississippi McCain Library & Archives.)

W.H. Jones Sr. was a prominent black teacher who recognized the opportunity for prosperity and change that could be offered through education. He was the primary motivation behind the establishment of a modern-day educational facility for the black community, and in 1921 his vision was realized with the opening of Eureka School. Jones became the first of many exemplary administrators at the school, and W.H. Jones Elementary School was later named in his honor. (Photograph courtesy of the University of Southern Mississippi McCain Library & Archives.)

This is a photograph of the Eureka School around 1921, when the facility first opened. The two-story brick school housed large classrooms for first through twelfth grades and also had an auditorium. Originally, there was no cafeteria, so the home economics students made lunches for the student body in a kitchen separate from the building. The school continued until the 1980s, when newer schools were opened to better accommodate the growing needs of the Hattiesburg Public School District. Historically, Eureka played an important role in the prosperity of the black community in Hattiesburg. (Photograph courtesy of the University of Southern Mississippi McCain Library & Archives.)

Five

CAMP SHELBY

It can be conjectured that Hattiesburg's central location, along with its citizens' fervent nationalism, was influential in attracting to the area the establishment of one of the largest military training installations in the United States. Located just 10 miles south of Hattiesburg, Camp Shelby was activated on July 18, 1917, to train a portion of the 37th Division and the 38th Division (nicknamed the "Cyclone Division" because of a tornado that swept through camp during training) for World War I. The leading sites for an Army base in Mississippi were Biloxi and Meridian, but the determining officer, Gen. Leonard Wood, met with Dr. Walter Wesley Crawford of Hattiesburg and Dr. George McHenry of Stone County, Atlanta, earlier in the year and was persuaded to consider Hattiesburg as a possibility. Several civic leaders were sponsored by the Hattiesburg Commerce Club to present the case for establishing the training facility near Hattiesburg. The delegation cited "good climate, railhead facilities, [and] ideal geography" in order to secure the site. After the good news was announced, Hattiesburg leaders wanted to name the base Camp Crawford, in light of Dr. Crawford's tireless efforts. In the end, though, the enlisted men chose the name. The 38th Division, which included many Kentuckians, chose to name the camp after Isaac Shelby, the famed Indian fighter, Revolutionary War hero, and first governor of Kentucky.

Today, Camp Shelby encompasses more than 134,820 acres (206 square miles) and is one of the largest state-owned and -operated field-training sites in the United States. It serves as a training site for National Guardsmen and reservists from throughout the country, hosts as many as 100,000 personnel annually, and is home to Mississippi's state military history museum, the Mississippi Armed Forces Museum.

Isaac Shelby garnered many accolades during the Revolutionary War, particularly during the Battle of King's Mountain in 1780. After the war, he was wildly popular throughout his home state of Kentucky, where he twice served as governor (1792–1796 and 1812–1816). During his second term as Kentucky's governor, he raised and took personal command of a force of 3,500 men in order to aid future president William Henry Harrison in defeating British forces at the Battle of the Thames in 1813. In 1817, he was presented a Congressional Gold Medal for his efforts. The soldiers of the 38th Division, who mostly came from Kentucky, named the military installation founded south of Hattiesburg in honor of Governor Shelby. (Photograph courtesy of the Mississippi Armed Forces Museum.)

These two panoramic views depict soldiers' lives at Camp Shelby as they prepare for deployment to France during World War I. The view at top, from around 1918, shows hundreds of soldiers from the 38th Division sitting behind their gear as they await a routine field inspection. The 38th Division, also known as the "Cyclone Division" because of a tornado that swept through the base during training, was among the first to be trained at Camp Shelby. Horse-drawn supply wagons are visible to the far left, and temporary housing—colloquially called a "tent city"—can be seen nestled among the pines at the top of the photograph. The image at bottom affords a better view of the soldiers' quartering areas. The two water towers (upper left) provided the soldiers with potable water. (Photograph courtesy of the Mississippi Armed Forces Museum.)

Camp Shelby's train depot is clearly visible to the left in this c. 1918 panoramic view. The railroad is one of the primary reasons the US military chose to locate Camp Shelby in such proximity to Hattiesburg. Railway access provided much-needed supplies to the training base and could accommodate entire divisions of soldiers ready for deployment. The eight-car garage (front, left) housing Ford Model Ts provided officers and training staff mobility over the camp's vast acreage. As evidenced in the following photograph, Camp Shelby was known for the tidy and sanitary condition of its tent cities. (Photograph courtesy of the Mississippi Armed Forces Museum.)

The 113th Engineer Battalion produced the *Souvenir Castle* booklet—copies of which were popular keepsakes for the entire 38th Division—to document its time and experience training at Camp Shelby. The 113th Engineer Battalion was the best-documented unit at Camp Shelby. *Souvenir Castle* contains photographs and descriptions of 17,000 men assembled for inspection, views of the camp from Regimental Headquarters, and images of "the canvas covered homes of the boys." Telegraph lines are clearly visible above the tent city, marking an important technological advancement. The 113th Engineers were deployed to the Breton Peninsula in France in September 1918 and were instrumental in the construction of a large base camp near the city of Brest. Later that year, they were sent to Konz, Germany, where they served in the Army of Occupation. (Photograph courtesy of the Mississippi Armed Forces Museum.)

Holding true to the Everybody Welcome sign perched on its roof, the Knights of Columbus (KOC) Hall at Camp Shelby provided a gathering place for soldiers stationed there. Though primarily a Catholic men's charity, the KOC put on dances and other social event, and, to this day, remains a staunch supporter of veterans of the US armed forces. (Photograph courtesy of the Mississippi Armed Forces Museum.)

Six-man huts were prefabricated and brought in by train and truck. They could be erected in 25 minutes and were easily retracted in good weather—an important feature that permitted sunlight into the soldiers' tents and likely contributed to the cleanliness of the camp. Camp Shelby had the best sanitation records of all US military training sites, a remarkable feat given the subtropical climate of South Mississippi. (Photograph courtesy of the Mississippi Armed Forces Museum.)

During World War I, division commander General Sage operated primarily out of this location. This building was centrally located in the camp at this time. Though not visible in this photograph, a bandstand with a bullhorn was positioned in front of the building so that the general could address a large assembly. The 38th Division Headquarters was dismantled after World War I. (Photograph courtesy of the Mississippi Armed Forces Museum.)

The camp's quartermaster building was located near the 38th Division Headquarters. Supplies and repairs were requisitioned through the quartermaster. (Photograph courtesy of the Mississippi Armed Forces Museum.)

The Camp Shelby Remount Depot might have seemed like scene out of the Wild West, complete with professional cowboys and mule skinners. Horses, mules, and wagons were still widely used during World War I; most officers were assigned horses, and artillery and supplies were often brought in on horse- or mule-drawn wagons. The Remount Depot centralized the care of the animals and kept riding tack and other equipment in good repair. (Photograph courtesy of the Mississippi Armed Forces Museum.)

Due to Camp Shelby's location 12 miles from downtown Hattiesburg, it was impractical for soldiers to slip away for a few hours to catch a show in town. The Camp Shelby Vaudeville Theatre provided a much-needed entertainment outlet for troops stationed there during World War I. A number of vaudeville troupes performed here and, as the marquee states, offered "an entire change of programe" twice a week. (Photograph courtesy of the Mississippi Armed Forces Museum.)

INFANTRY ON THE MARCH---CAMP SHELBY NEAR HATTIESBURG, MISS.

This postcard shows Camp Shelby's typical World War I–era training and its characteristic pine trees in the background. The picture started as a black-and-white photograph and was water-colored before mass reproduction. The postcard shows infantrymen on the march, either to quarters or training—an exercise conducted with grueling regularity. (Photograph courtesy of the Mississippi Armed Forces Museum.)

"Kentucky" Machine Gun Detachment, Camp Shelby, Hattiesburg, Miss.

Soldiers train to fire British-made Lewis machine guns from the prone position. Machine guns represented a new technology, and soldiers with this specialized training operated as detachments from the regular infantry. Divisions were often nicknamed according to the states from which they hailed. These soldiers came from Kentucky, as did the majority of soldiers belonging to the famed 38th Division. (Photograph courtesy of the Mississippi Armed Forces Museum.)

These unidentified medical personnel from Camp Shelby Base Hospital are pictured in front of a field tent. (Photograph courtesy of the Mississippi Armed Forces Museum.)

In this view of the Camp Shelby Base Hospital, the top buildings farthest in the background served as nurses' quarters, and the building on the right functioned as the receiving ward. (Photograph courtesy of the Mississippi Armed Forces Museum.)

This picture shows another view of Camp Shelby Base Hospital. The structure in the foreground is an administration building, and directly behind it stands a laboratory. The main operating facility can be seen jutting out slightly behind the laboratory. (Photograph courtesy of the Mississippi Armed Forces Museum.)

The main road that runs through the middle of the Camp Shelby Base Hospital is prominently featured in this photograph. The building in the foreground, to the right of the road, served as a recuperating ward for officers. Behind it is a recuperating ward for soldiers returning home from the front line in France. The structures on the left side of the street served the same function. (Photograph courtesy of the Mississippi Armed Forces Museum.)

The c. 1918 picture at top shows the newly constructed Camp Shelby Base Hospital, which had 500 beds and was staffed with both military and civilian medical personnel. Dr. Walter Wesley Crawford—who had been instrumental in attracting the establishment of Camp Shelby in

The extensive medical staff of the Camp Shelby Base Hospital consisted of the Army Medical Corps and the Army Nurses Corps and was supplemented by contracted civilian nurses, surgeons, and orderlies. In 1918, more than 12,000 noncommissioned nurses served at US stations worldwide.

Hattiesburg—served as chief surgeon here from 1917 until he was deployed to serve in the same capacity at Base Hospital 79 in Verdun, France. The image directly above is a contemporary view of the same area. (Photographs courtesy of the Mississippi Armed Forces Museum.)

Though they were not allotted officer status during the war, Congress eventually granted them "relative rank." Their pay, however, remained less than that of a man with equal rank. (Photograph courtesy of the Mississippi Armed Forces Museum.)

Bart, Lapp, and myself in front of barracks, Camp Shelby, Miss.

Instead of being sent to the main infirmary at Camp Shelby Base Hospital, soldiers with minor injuries—such as sprains or breaks—were often treated at the Barracks Medical Detachment. The barracks were staffed with military medics primarily trained in first aid and battlefield trauma care, rather than full-fledged physicians. (Photograph courtesy of the Mississippi Armed Forces Museum.)

The Camp Shelby Library provided soldiers with ample reading material during their time in Hattiesburg. The American Library Association established 36 camp libraries, provided library collections to over 500 locations (including military hospitals), raised over $5 million, and distributed between seven million and ten million books and magazines as part of its Library War Service program. (Photograph courtesy of the Mississippi Armed Forces Museum.)

Their training completed, the 151st Infantry Regiment (primarily consisting of soldiers from Indiana) leaves Camp Shelby via train on June 4, 1918. The regiment, with its motto "Wide Awake! Wide Awake," was deployed to France. (Photograph courtesy of the Mississippi Armed Forces Museum.)

Each soldier was subjected to regular inspections and was responsible for maintaining his uniform. They were therefore allotted time each day to mend and wash their garments. This photograph shows soldiers, their sleeves rolled up, hand-washing their own uniforms outdoors with washboards and metal tubs. (Photograph courtesy of the Mississippi Armed Forces Museum.)

Soldiers chop and stack wood in the South Mississippi heat under the gaze of guards armed with standard military-issue M1903 Springfield rifles. Soldiers that committed minor offences were placed under detention and, as part of their punishment, were often used around the camp to perform various forms of hard labor. (Photograph courtesy of the Mississippi Armed Forces Museum.)

Above, the kitchen staff makes ready to prepare a feast, and below, soldiers enjoy various delicacies during Christmas dinner in one of Camp Shelby's many mess halls. Decorations can be seen hanging overhead. Though extraneous niceties were not regularly afforded to the soldiers, the military made significant efforts to make the men feel at home during the holidays. (Photographs courtesy of the Mississippi Armed Forces Museum.)

View of the Ky. Street Squaw Camp- Camp Shelby, MS 1917

Wives of officers and civilian doctors were allotted the rustic convenience of "Squaw Camp" housing during World War I (above). The area is now of great archaeological interest, and public excavations are frequently held at the site (below). (Photographs courtesy of the Mississippi Armed Forces Museum.)

An unidentified officer sits on the porch of a cabin in the Squaw Camp with his son and the family dog. These dwellings were built fast of rough-hewn lumber—note that the porch columns are not debarked. Though bereft of modern conveniences like running water or electricity, the Squaw Camp provided families of officers and civilian "doctors" slightly better accommodations than those found in the tent cities. (Photograph courtesy of the Mississippi Armed Forces Museum.)

Two unidentified officers keep their wives company outside of the Squaw Camp. (Photograph courtesy of the Mississippi Armed Forces Museum.)

"Kentucky" Division Bakery, Camp Shelby, Hattiesburg, Miss.

"Kentucky" 149th Inf. Band. Camp Shelby, Hattiesburg, Miss.

Depicted here are two features that were common to each Camp Shelby regiment. The top image is the bakery. American soldiers were known as doughboys abroad, and the term is thought to be a reference to one of their staple food items, for their meals almost always included biscuits and doughnuts, or "fried dough." At the bottom is a regimental band. Each regiment had a band or small orchestra, which allowed for occasional musical performances. (Photograph courtesy of the Mississippi Armed Forces Museum.)

"Indiana Kitchen" (so called because many soldiers in the 38th Division were from Indiana) was one of the field mess areas at Camp Shelby that served soldiers training away from the main mess halls. Food service in the field posed a number of logistical and hygienic problems—many answered with the use of a simple open-air tent. (Photograph courtesy of the Mississippi Armed Forces Museum.)

A soldier poses with local children. Many soldiers stationed at Camp Shelby during World War I came from all-white communities outside of Mississippi and while on training maneuvers were exposed to black children for the first time. It was such a novel experience (for both the children and the soldier) that many soldiers would make a point of having their pictures taken. (Photograph courtesy of the Mississippi Armed Forces Museum.)

The 152nd Ambulance Corps was the first unit to arrive at Camp Shelby in 1917. The "Sanitary Train" was made up of four ambulance companies with 12 ambulances each, a medical supply unit, and four mobile field hospitals (each set up to treat gas-related injuries, surgery, or ordinary illnesses) and included around 100 officers and over 1,000 enlisted men under the command of the division surgeon. (Photograph courtesy of the Mississippi Armed Forces Museum.)

The Selective Service Act of 1917 authorized the federal government to conscript able-bodied men to fight in World War I. The act outlined the Army's structure as consisting of the regular Army, the National Guard, and the National Army (consisting of draftee and volunteer divisions). The typical National Army uniform, as seen here, featured an old-fashioned campaign hat (worn until World War I), the 1903 Springfield rifle, and puttees (leg wrappings that offered protection against barbed wire). (Photograph courtesy of the Mississippi Armed Forces Museum.)

Six

CITY LIFE

On Thanksgiving Day 1912, two events signified Hattiesburg's boom. It was the day of both the city's first college football game at Kamper Park and the adoption of the "Hub City" moniker. The lighting of the five-story Hub City sign in downtown Hattiesburg was described in the *Hattiesburg News*:

> "Hattiesburg the Hub" will be a central revolving set of lights; and from this center, lights arranged as spokes will lead out to circular groups of light, indicating the three ports of New Orleans, Gulfport and Mobile, with Natchez on the west, Vicksburg northwest, Jackson north, and Meridian northeast, the idea contemplating two wheels revolving in opposite directions, with "Hattiesburg the Hub" ever in the blazing center of light.

By this time, most of the city streets were paved, and a municipal waterworks was up and running on Front and Forrest Streets. The Hattiesburg Traction Company streetcars provided transportation for locals. Industry was on the rise, and many residents were experiencing the thrill of the automobile for the first time. Hattiesburg was in full bloom.

This momentum would, naturally, wane. The area's timberland was being depleted at an alarming rate, and skidder logging—which used massive winches to drag logs to the railway tracks and thereby destroyed new growth—prohibited the sustainability of the forests. By 1930, most of the sawmills were shut down. Camp Shelby was deactivated as a federal installation from 1918 to 1934, and the decline of Hattiesburg's two biggest employers of the era would unfortunately coincide with the onset of the Great Depression, leaving the once thriving town struggling to avoid stagnation.

The city endured. Though the timber was depleted, Camp Shelby was reactivated with the United States' entry into World War II, and the country clawed its way out of the Depression. Many of the existing businesses in Hattiesburg would find a way to suffer through the hard times, and eventually, new industries would emerge. The following pictures represent a distinct brand of optimism and a generation who, though they had lived in a boomtown before it experienced its first big bust, remained unbridled by defeat.

Front Street looking South from Palace Restaurant, Hattiesburg, Miss.

This early downtown scene is of Front Street, looking south from the Palace Restaurant. It is reminiscent of an old-west town with its dirt streets and horse-and-buggy modes of transportation. Visible too are the first power lines in downtown Hattiesburg. Many of these early buildings still stand, and the Front Street area remains commercially vital. (Photograph courtesy of the University of Southern Mississippi McCain Library & Archives.)

This is another c. 1900 view of Front Street businesses, featuring Katz Clothiers and the Independent Order of Odd Fellows building. The latter, interestingly, is one of the oldest buildings in Hattiesburg, and the fraternal organization that it housed was founded in the United States in 1819. The building has recently been restored and now features gallery space for Hattiesburg artists. (Photograph courtesy of the University of Southern Mississippi McCain Library & Archives.)

Riding high on a surge of optimism that stemmed from Hattiesburg's unchecked economic growth, the Commercial Club sponsored a contest to give the young city an attractive slogan. Local businessman R.R. Swittenburg came up with the winning entry, "the Hub City," which firmly marked Hattiesburg's geographic centrality and railroad access as an attraction for new industries. The Hub City sign—measuring 42 feet in diameter and using 1,142 lightbulbs—was erected atop the five-story Ross Building, just a stone's throw from the Hattiesburg Railway Depot, in November 1912. It would be lit nightly, from dusk until midnight, for the next 35 years. (Photograph courtesy of the University of Southern Mississippi McCain Library & Archives.)

In this eastward view down Front Street, the back of Hattiesburg's famous Hub City sign, which greets visitors as they arrive at the train depot, is visible to the right. Though the iconic sign has been absent from Hattiesburg for many decades, there is currently an effort to replicate it in the same location. (Photograph courtesy of the University of Southern Mississippi McCain Library & Archives.)

This pamphlet, generated by the Hattiesburg Chamber of Commerce, uses the Hub City logo to celebrate the city and surrounding areas. The pamphlet recounts the general health of the community, with particular regards to industry, agriculture, and politics. (Photograph courtesy of the University of Southern Mississippi McCain Library & Archives.)

Quint Orr is seen here at the wheel of his Stanley Steamer automobile on the streets of Hattiesburg. To the right, observers with more rudimentary forms of transportation (a bicycle and a horse-drawn wagon) look on in amazement. This was one of the first automobiles in Hattiesburg. (Photograph courtesy of the University of Southern Mississippi McCain Library & Archives.)

This photograph was originally titled *Pat's Ford* by its owner. It depicts a Hattiesburg family riding around town in style in an early Ford Model T, a familiar sight in at the time. Model T vehicles were rare in Hattiesburg, so when a family member acquired one, usually all wanted a ride. (Photograph courtesy of the University of Southern Mississippi McCain Library & Archives.)

This is a rare photograph of Ed Howell, a prominent, early black businessman, driving a horse and buggy with his dog on Fifth Street. His home was located nearby on the corner of Jackson and Fifth Streets. Three children can be seen standing on the sidewalk. Howell was assassinated in 1907 at the People's Bank on Mobile Street, which he founded and owned. (Photograph courtesy of the Deborah Denard Delgado family.)

This photograph depicts what is believed to be the first commercial vehicle in Hattiesburg. Owned by Standard Oil, it is being proudly displayed by an employee, Jessie Collier, with his two small children, Jessie Jr. and Vera, seated inside. (Photograph courtesy of the University of Southern Mississippi McCain Library & Archives.)

Taken between about 1910 and 1913, this photograph of a Mr. and Mrs. Favre of Gulfport, Mississippi, driving their early automobile, reveals the beautiful homes of a Hattiesburg neighborhood. (Photograph courtesy of the University of Southern Mississippi McCain Library & Archives.)

Carl Autry, a Hattiesburg police officer from around 1910 to 1920, was proud to be the first officer issued a motorcycle with which to patrol the city. (Photograph courtesy of the University of Southern Mississippi McCain Library & Archives.)

This image captures a horse-drawn parade float for Hattiesburg Furniture Company on Main Street. Annotations on the photograph identify F.H. Waggoner and Lurlyne Collier as being among the several children riding. Leaning against the float for the photo opportunity is a well-dressed businessman. (Photograph courtesy of the University of Southern Mississippi McCain Library & Archives.)

Five female students of the Mississippi Normal College board the trolley car for transportation. (Photograph courtesy of the University of Southern Mississippi McCain Library & Archives.)

Here is another example of an early-model automobile in Hattiesburg. This one is located at Camp Shelby, and a uniformed officer poses beside it. The front license plate reading PHS US 2 indicates that it may be a Public Health Service vehicle used during the influenza outbreak of 1918. (Photograph courtesy of the University of Southern Mississippi McCain Library & Archives.)

A young woman identified as Elbert Cooper is seen trying to hand crank a Ford Model T on the side of the street in a Hattiesburg neighborhood in this 1920s photograph. (Photograph courtesy of the University of Southern Mississippi McCain Library & Archives.)

The Hattiesburg Saenger Theater is among several of its type in the South, with others found in Biloxi, New Orleans, Mobile, and Pensacola, to name a few. This theater opened on Thanksgiving Day 1929, and admissions were 6¢ a feature. The Saenger Theater is believed to be the first structure in Hattiesburg to have air-conditioning. (Photograph courtesy of Brooke Cruthirds.)

This photograph, thought to show a c. 1920 Fourth of July parade, features several men riding in a flatbed vehicle and waving US flags. They surround a man dressed as Uncle Sam. (Photograph courtesy of the University of Southern Mississippi McCain Library & Archives.)

Many outfits did not have enough horses to draw their cargo, so they equipped their wagons with oxen instead. Here, a civilian rides up front with two officers from nearby Camp Shelby along an upscale area of Hattiesburg. Another man can be seen riding in the back of the wagon (Photograph courtesy of the University of Southern Mississippi McCain Library & Archives.)

Horses were costly to purchase and maintain, and hard to come by during the war effort. Here, the innovative driver has harnessed a team of goats to pull him through a residential Hattiesburg neighborhood. (Photograph courtesy of the Mississippi Armed Forces Museum.)

In this unique view, a team of goats pulls a small buggy for these children as they play together in a middle-class neighborhood. (Photograph courtesy of the Mississippi Armed Forces Museum.)

Founded in 1901, the Hattiesburg Ice & Coal Company is still in business over a century later. Ralph "Rab" Lewis, along with two teenage helpers, is seen here in an upscale Hattiesburg neighborhood next to a horse-drawn ice wagon. One of the helpers is holding a holding a block of ice with tongs. City dwellers could order up to 100 pounds of ice blocks cut in 25-pound increments and have it delivered directly to their iceboxes. Note the early phone number (144) advertised on the side of the commercial cart. (Photograph courtesy of the University of Southern Mississippi McCain Library & Archives.)

This early-1900s photograph of South Bay Street indicates a progression in transportation within Hattiesburg. Trolley cars can be seen running alongside horse-drawn buggies through the residential area. Power lines are also visible lining the street. (Photograph courtesy of the University of Southern Mississippi McCain Library & Archives.)

In this 1920s view of Bay Street, a lone early automobile is parked in front of a home in an upscale residential area. Children can be seen playing in the front yard, and a landscaped median is also evident in the photograph. (Photograph courtesy of the University of Southern Mississippi McCain Library & Archives.)

This photograph was taken at the family home of David W. White Sr. and his wife, Lula Britton White, located on Fourth Street. Pictured are Lula's mother, Hattie Austin Britton, and children Margaret Britton Hendrix (left), Leon Britton Jr. (center), and David W. White Jr. The Whites were a prominent Hattiesburg family. (Photograph courtesy of the Deborah Denard Delgado family.)

This photograph features another lovely structure on Bay Street around the 1920s. The Forrest Club was located at 205 Bay Street and was a venue for many social and civic activities in the community, including dances, parties, vocational training sessions, and more. The site was later converted into the Hulett-Winstead Funeral Home. (Photograph courtesy of the University of Southern Mississippi McCain Library & Archives.)

An unidentified family rests in the shade of their front porch—a popular Southern pastime. This spacious home features a wide porch for a swing and rocking chairs shaded further by Boston ferns. (Photograph courtesy of the University of Southern Mississippi McCain Library & Archives.)

A family poses around 1910 on the front steps of their ornate residence. Husband, wife, mother-in-law, and three young females are featured with their pet dog and bunny. (Photograph courtesy of the Deborah Denard Delgado family.)

A mother and grandmother pose here on the steps of their Hattiesburg home with a young boy. This house is raised off the ground as a precaution against the floodwaters that were common in the area during storms. The home also features large Boston ferns to help shade the porch from the sweltering sun. (Photograph courtesy of the Mississippi Armed Forces Museum.)

This unusual photograph depicts a "Tom Thumb wedding." The large, formal wedding party consisted entirely of youngsters, with Willetta Smith and Dudley Conner acting as the bride and groom. (Conner can also be seen on page 125.) The soiree took place at the Hattiesburg Opera House around 1910 complete with a somber-looking pastor presiding over the festivities. (Photograph courtesy of the University of Southern Mississippi McCain Library & Archives.)

These two young ladies are in their Sunday finest for a professional portrait session. Their ornate dress is typical of the 1920s, with fine hats, floral decoration, and stylistic stitchery. The ladies are identified "Grandma Clara" and "Aunt Nette." (Photograph courtesy of the Deborah Denard Delgado family.)

This Halloween masquerade party was held at the Forrest Club at 205 Bay Street around 1913. The participants appear to all be adults, and a variety of costumes are represented. (Photograph courtesy of the University of Southern Mississippi McCain Library & Archives.)

This early image is of Hattiesburg's first Mardi Gras Ball, hosted by the Mystic Krewe of Zeus. Seen here on March 13, 1924 are the Krewe's King and Queen with their royal court. Mardi Gras has a rich history in the Southern region of the United States, and the Krewe of Zeus still celebrates in Hattiesburg each year with elaborate and lavish displays of wealth. (Photograph courtesy of the University of Southern Mississippi McCain Library & Archives.)

In this c. 1927 photograph, the band of Hattiesburg's Leaf River Chapter of the Woodmen of the World poses on the steps of the Forrest County Courthouse. The Woodmen of the World was a benevolent fraternal organization formed in 1890 to help young pioneer families become financially independent. (Photograph courtesy of the University of Southern Mississippi McCain Library & Archives.)

This panoramic view captures an important mood as tens of thousands of Hattiesburg residents gather to celebrate the end of World War I in 1919. People hold banners and flags and gather to hear speeches announcing the details of the long-awaited end of the war. The massive crowd

The Forrest County Courthouse, built in 1908 in the Neoclassical Revival style popular at the time, served as the seat of government for the newly formed county. The building underwent a major remodel in 1922 and a $6.2 million renovation in 1998, and is in the National Register of Historic Places. (Photograph courtesy of the University of Southern Mississippi McCain Library & Archives.)

is assembled near the Southern Railway, not far from Main and Newman Streets. (Photograph courtesy of the University of Southern Mississippi McCain Library & Archives.)

These two scenes are from a c. 1905 flood. Bay Street is submerged in water, and stranded women and children are seen on the left, waiting to be ferried across by men in canoes. Three men and two women are seen canoeing through the flooded area. Violent storms in the forms of hurricanes and tornadoes bring tremendous damages. (Photographs courtesy of the University of Southern Mississippi McCain Library & Archives.)

Oaklawn Cemetery was founded before Hattiesburg was even declared a city, and its gate was erected in 1887. Many prominent Hattiesburg residents are buried here, including former governors Paul B. Johnson Sr. and Paul B. Johnson Jr.; prominent businessman and engineer George Komp; Jesse Collier Sr.; Dudley Conner and his wife, Lorene; influential doctor Wesley Walter Crawford; lumber magnate, railroad man, and William Carey University benefactor W.S.F. Tatum; and noted educators W.I. Thames and George L. Hawkins. (Photographs courtesy of Brooke Cruthirds.)

16. John Wood's photograph of Sullivan, probably the most popular picture ever taken of the champion (1885) (William Schutte Collection)

John Wood's 1895 photograph of John L. Sullivan shows the famed bare-knuckle champion at his peak. Standing five feet, ten and a half inches tall and weighing 195 pounds, the "Boston Strong Boy" lived life with gusto, smoking black cigars, drinking bourbon out of beer steins, and indulging a legendary appetite. Sullivan, born of Irish-immigrant parents, began boxing at the age of 19 and won the bare-knuckle championship from Paddy Ryan in 1882 at the age of 24. He was dubbed by fans in his hometown of Boston as "the Great John L." and would tour the world with a standing offer of $1,000 to any white man—he was openly racist and refused to face any man of color in the ring—who could last four rounds with him. (Photograph courtesy of the University of Southern Mississippi McCain Library & Archives.)

On December 7, 1888, John Sullivan issued a handwritten letter challenging Jake Kilrain to a fight, "according to the latest rules of the London prize ring." The rules dictated that the fighters did not wear gloves, that wrestling was allowed, that a round lasted until one fighter was knocked down, and that the fight would continue until one fighter was unable to get up from the floor under his own power. Each side agreed to post a winner-take-all $10,000 side bet, though it can be conjectured that bragging rights were far more valuable to these fighters than any purse. (Photograph courtesy of the University of Southern Mississippi McCain Library & Archives.)

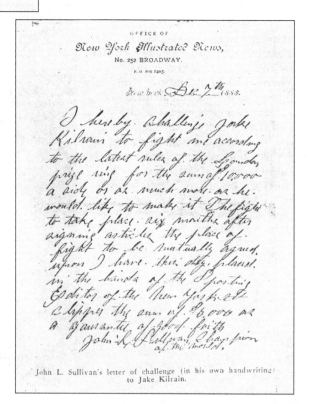

John L. Sullivan's letter of challenge (in his own handwriting) to Jake Kilrain.

The fight was the result of a public feud between Sullivan and newspaperman Richard K. Fox. Sullivan had snubbed Fox at a Boston saloon in the early 1880s, motivating Fox to find a fighter capable of deflating the champion's ego. He took interest in John Joseph Kilrain, who had honed his fighting skills against mill workers in his hometown of Somerville, Massachusetts, and goaded Sullivan into a fight by publishing that the champion was afraid to face off against Kilrain. After first seeing Kilrain fight Jem Smith to a draw in a 106-round bout, Fox declared Kilrain the heavyweight champion and fitted him with a silver, diamond-studded championship belt. The tactics eventually worked, and the fight was set to take place a few miles outside of Hattiesburg, Mississippi. (Photograph courtesy of the University of Southern Mississippi McCain Library & Archives.)

23. Jake Kilrain (about 1889) (William Schutte Collection)

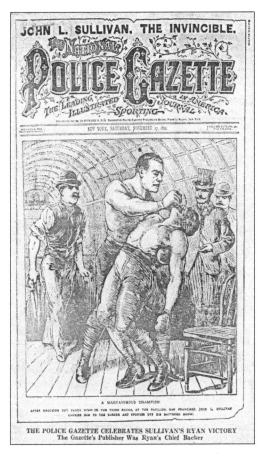

JOHN L. SULLIVAN. THE INVINCIBLE.

THE NATIONAL

POLICE GAZETTE

THE LEADING ILLUSTRATED SPORTING JOURNAL IN AMERICA.

NEW YORK, SATURDAY, NOVEMBER 17, 1886.

A MAGNANIMOUS CHAMPION.

AFTER KNOCKING OUT PADDY RYAN IN THE THIRD ROUND, AT THE PAVILION, SAN FRANCISCO, JOHN L. SULLIVAN CARRIES HIM TO THE CORNER AND SPONGES OFF HIS BATTERED BROW.

THE POLICE GAZETTE CELEBRATES SULLIVAN'S RYAN VICTORY
The Gazette's Publisher Was Ryan's Chief Backer

Though this *Police Gazette* sketch depicts John L. Sullivan as the "Magnanimous Champion," it provides further insight into Fox's grudge against the fighter. Note the text at the bottom, which indicates that the defeated Paddy Ryan was backed by Fox himself. Arranging and promoting the bout between Sullivan and Kilrain was a long-term project of Fox's; the sketch appeared four years after the Ryan-Sullivan fight, and three years before Sullivan would take on Kilrain. (Photograph courtesy of the University of Southern Mississippi McCain Library & Archives.)

The one-story clapboard house that Jake Kilrain stayed in before the fight belonged to Col. Charles W. Rich, one of the fights primary promoters. Though the precise location is disputed, the fight is most commonly believed to have taken place on a hill behind this house. (Photograph courtesy of the University of Southern Mississippi McCain Library & Archives.)

The ring was between 16 and 24 square feet, constructed of two cords of rope strung between eight wooden posts. The bleachers, built specifically for this event, were made of rough-hewn yellow pine that reportedly oozed resin in the July heat. Famed Dodge City lawman and gunslinger William Barclay "Bat" Masterson acted as timekeeper. (Photograph courtesy of the University of Southern Mississippi McCain Library & Archives.)

The governors of both Louisiana and Mississippi actively sought to prevent the fight from happening, but to no avail. Mississippi governor Robert Lowry sent Marion County sheriff W.J. Cowart to put an end to the competition. Cowart undoubtedly carried out his orders as well as the situation would allow; before the event commenced, he stepped into the middle of the ring and attempted to read Governor Lowry's edict to shut down the fight. After being booed by the crowd of over 3,000 men, the sheriff smiled and said that he had other business to attend to. The fight was widely discussed for years to come and was often used in advertisements, such as this notice for a New Orleans shoe shop. (Photograph courtesy of the University of Southern Mississippi McCain Library & Archives.)

John L. Sullivan defeated Jake Kilrain in the 75-round fight that lasted two hours and sixteen minutes. By the end, both Kilrain and Sullivan were a vision of carnage—a mess of broken noses, swollen hands, blackened eyes, and bloodied ears—but it was Kilrain's cornerman who stopped the fight when he threw a sponge into the ring at the beginning of the 75th round. The ring was disassembled, the ring posts were splintered, and the ropes were cut into pieces and sold to souvenir-hungry spectators. Both men were tried and convicted for prizefighting, and each was ordered to pay a $500 fine. In later years, Sullivan and Kilrain would tour the vaudeville circuit together, putting on exhibition bouts. (Photograph courtesy of Brooke Cruthirds.)

A few miles outside the booming city of Hattiesburg, a man sits on the front steps of his one-room cabin, surrounded only by the natural resources of the Piney Woods. A white draft horse (judging by the harness) is tied to a tree to the left. (Photograph courtesy of the University of Southern Mississippi McCain Library & Archives.)

Seven

RURAL SCENES

How things change, and how they stay the same! All the hustle and bustle that took place inside Hub City's limits could easily be forgotten with a quick country drive. To the delight of many, the hinterlands of Hattiesburg did not have all the accoutrements—or the burdens—of city life. In the early part of the 20th century, running water was provided not by the city but by the Bouie or Leaf Rivers or any number of creeks that marbled the landscape. Outhouses were typical to a rural home, as were hand-dug wells and hand-operated pumps. Survival depended on hard work.

Houses were heated by wood-burning stoves or fireplaces, and light was provided by candles. Life outside the city seemed to exist in a temporal vacuum; not much had changed during the previous 50 years with regard to the day-to-day existence of those living on the fringes of Hattiesburg. While most townsfolk had power lines running directly to their residences by 1935, only one percent of Mississippi's rural farms and homes had electrical service. The expense of delivering power to the sparsely populated countryside was virtually insurmountable until the establishment of the Tennessee Valley Authority in 1933 and the Rural Electrification Act in 1936. The Rural Electrification Act provided federal money to facilitate the distribution of electricity to rural areas. Even so, some parts of Forrest and Lamar Counties were left in the dark (electrically) well into the 1950s.

Still, some people are not altogether opposed to letting certain things alone—or, at the least, letting change trickle in as slowly as possible. Mercifully, there are still some small corners of this part of the world that have been left relatively unaltered by the march of progress. One of the best things about living in the Hub City is that, just as it was a century ago, a quick drive in the right direction will take one away from the hustle and bustle of it all.

Teenage Margaret Britton Hendrix poses around the late 1920s at the point known as Twin Forks, the place where the Leaf and Bouie Rivers merge. Twin Forks was also a very early name for the Hattiesburg area before William Harris Hardy renamed it. (Photograph courtesy of the Deborah Denard Delgado family.)

In this 1920s photograph, a railroad truss can be seen spanning the Leaf River. The bridge was built in 1907 near Beaumont, Mississippi, and was placed in the National Register of Historic Places in 1988. The Leaf River is a principal tributary of the Pascagoula River and was used as a route to the Gulf of Mexico by the Choctaws of prehistory, the white trappers of the early 19th century, and the loggers of the mid- and late 19th century. (Photograph courtesy of the University of Southern Mississippi McCain Library & Archives.)

LEAF RIVER SCENE. HATTIESBURG. MISS.

This postcard bears a recolored photograph of the Leaf River by famed Hattiesburg photographer D.B. Henley. It predates 1908. (Photograph courtesy of the University of Southern Mississippi McCain Library & Archives.)

Views like these make it difficult to argue the appeal of a nice drive through the country. Jackson Highway connected Hattiesburg to Lumberton in the early part of the 20th century and likely was cut out of the pine forest to serve as a logging road between the two towns. Note the difference in undergrowth in these two photographs. In the image above, undergrowth is kept short by the canopy of established pines, while the recently cleared timberland seen below features lush undergrowth. A twisted young pine can be seen on the left side of the road—likely damaged by skidding, a process in which loggers would use long cables to pull logs out of the forest and to the railroad tracks. The big felled trees would, more often than not, suffer damage in the process. (Photographs courtesy of the University of Southern Mississippi McCain Library & Archives.)

Jackson Highway, Hattiesburg, Miss.

This set of photographs is included in a Mississippi Normal College scrapbook. In them, two couples are captured on a double date to the country on July 4, 1930. The sweethearts are seen happily posing next to the car parked along a grass-lined dirt road. The couple below is identified as "Elma and Walter," while the pair to the right is identified only as "Woody and me." (Photographs courtesy of the University of Southern Mississippi McCain Library & Archives.)

This c. 1930 photograph, captioned "Elma and me," documents the activities of a young Mississippi Normal College student who, in her spare time, enjoys taking up arms in a rural area outside of Hattiesburg. In it, two young women are seen holding their firearms in a wooded area and presumably enjoying a good hunt. (Photograph courtesy of the University of Southern Mississippi McCain Library & Archives.)

Few local foods were as favored among the troops serving at Camp Shelby as watermelon. Plentiful in South Mississippi, they are well documented in letters home and in photographs taken by soldiers between training exercises. (Photograph courtesy of the Mississippi Armed Forces Museum.)

Dudley Conner is held by his father on the bank of one of the mineral creeks of Rawls Springs. A longtime resident of Hattiesburg, Dudley and his wife are buried in Hattiesburg at Oaklawn Cemetery. (Photograph courtesy of the University of Southern Mississippi McCain Library & Archives.)

This 1920s photograph gives a sense of the majesty of the longleaf pine forests. The early motor vehicle is dwarfed by the surrounding trees as the driver winds his way along the dirt road. Joyride scenes such as this became common as more people began to acquire personal vehicles. (Photograph courtesy of the University of Southern Mississippi McCain Library & Archives.)

This 1930s aerial photograph provides a detailed glimpse at some of the more rural areas lying just outside of the city. Here, an early-model vehicle is stopped before a railroad track while passengers get out to inspect. In the background is a rural residence surrounded by farmland that has been tilled (on the left) and cut (on the right). Sharecropping, a system of leasing land from a landowner in exchange for a high percentage of the crops grown on the property, is still practiced in some parts of rural Mississippi today. (Photograph courtesy of the University of Southern Mississippi McCain Library & Archives.)

This aerial view shows the Highway 49 cloverleaf under construction, around the 1940s, near the present site of Cloverleaf Mall in Hattiesburg. The cloverleaf radiates in the four cardinal directions and, like the railway lines of the late 19th century, seems to mark Hattiesburg on the map with an X. (Photograph courtesy of the University of Southern Mississippi McCain Library & Archives.)

127

Visit us at
arcadiapublishing.com

CPSIA information can be obtained
at www.ICGtesting.com
Printed in the USA
LVHW060047180622
721531LV00007B/295